I0827886

Published April 2021

Typeface: Agnes. This font was found on the internet and did not come with a license. While we try to make sure that all the fonts on fontsquirrel.com are properly licensed for commercial use, there are many fonts that have either been abandoned by their authors or the authors distribute their fonts without an explicit license. It is our opinion that if the unlicensed font is freely available for download from either the original source or from multiple free-font sites then we assume it to be safe to use the font commercially. This is no guarantee of such freedom, but there are so many unlicensed free fonts distributed by primary sources that the intentions must be read that the font is free to use how you like.We are not lawyers and don't pretend to be them on TV. Please report any errors/violations you know of. http://www.fontsquirrel.com/contact

My name is Ryan, and this is my crew! I have four children, Eli who is 10, Aiden and Brady (the twins) who are 7, and Isabella who is now 2.

My wife April and I have spent the last six years building the animal rescue and educational facility into what it is today. (Aka. my wife's dream). You will meet them all in the books to come, however, these books are written for my daughter Isabella. She is growing up side-by-side with all of these animals on a daily basis. The stories that I tell are just memories and experiences written for all to see. Isabella is living, helping and loving animals alongside her mom each day. I am excited to be able to share a little of my life (our life) with the world.

~Ryan Cicchelli

Hey guys!

My name is

Isabella!

I am 2 1/2

years old!

What is

your

name?

I live in Northern Michigan!

Right where the heart is!

Where do you live?

My entire family

loves animals

and so do I!

I bet you do too!

We work with animals from around the whole world- Africa, Asia and even Australia!

Some animals have special needs and they come here to have a better life. I get to help my parents care for all of them!

Some animals outgrow educational programs and some just need a new home as they get older. Have you ever moved to a new place?

When I grow up

I would really love to work with animals. I want to rescue them, just like my mom!

I help mom do chores every day. We feed and water all the animals, and make sure everyone's messes are cleaned up! What ways do you help at home?

I love feeding the animals with my mom. We always stop and spend time with every animal! I always say "hi!" and give them snacks while mom makes sure everyone is happy!

It is fun growing up with all the animals, but a lot of work.

In the spring I even get to help with injured or orphaned wildlife!

I help bottle feed fawns,

fix broken wings,

and raise baby raccoons!

After we help them get better

and grow big and strong,

we release them

back into the wild!

Some days

I help

check

on hurt

animals

that need

help!

Some days

I help my daddy

build new enclosures

and drive the back hoe!

What have you helped

your parents build?

I love when he

lets me drive!

I hope you get to visit me

and all my friends one day!

I bet you would love them all

as much as I do!

Come and see us soon!

Isabella's Scrapbook

I can't wait for you to meet

my friends in the next books!

MISSION STATEMENT

My passion and love for animals began when I was just a little girl. Every animal that crossed my path I was always trying to befriend or help, and since growing up, not much has changed. I began rescuing wildlife in my early adult years, we have successfully rehabbed 100s of injured and orphaned wildlife, returning them to the wild once they are healthy and strong. As our rescue has grown, we began working more and more with exotic animals from all parts of world, that have been raised in captivity. My love for animals as a child has grown from passion, to commitment, to dedication. Here at Cicchelli Second Chance Rescue & Exotics it is our mission to build a legacy for our children while committing to the unknown. Committing to animals in need before we even know the situation and continuing to help and provide the best possible care to every animal that calls our facility home.

April Cicchelli, Co-Founder

www.ingramcontent.com/pod-product-compliance
Lightning Source LLC
LaVergne TN
LVHW052303100826
845147LV00001B/128